Keith Brumpton

LOOK OUT, LOCH NESS MONSTER!

MACDONALD YOUNG BOOKS

this book is dedicated
to little monsters everywhere

Thank·you to Nessie
who was kind enough to keep
still while I drew her.

£3.99

This book is to be returned on or before
the last date stamped below.

EDUCATIONAL LIBRARY SERVICE
AUCHTERDERRAN CENTRE
Woodend Road
Cardenden
Fife KY5 0NE
Tel 01592 414611

A very boring bit of the book which no-one ever reads.

First published in Great Britain in 1992
by Simon & Schuster Young Books

Reprinted in 1992, 1993 and 1994

Reprinted in 1995 by
Macdonald Young Books Ltd
Campus 400
Maylands Avenue
Hemel Hempstead
Herts HP2 7EZ

Photoset in 16/22pt Meridien by Goodfellow & Egan Ltd, Cambridge
Colour origination by Scantrans Pte Ltd, Singapore

Printed and bound in Portugal by Ediçoes ASA

British Library Cataloguing in Publication Data available

ISBN 0 7500 1071 1
ISBN 0 7500 1072 X pbk

Chapter One

LOCH NESS
NO BATHING

ZZZ

dozing hedgehog

Loch Ness is a huge dark lake in the north of
Scotland, deep as a giant's pockets, and
surrounded on all sides by pine trees and
forest.

Some people claim that in the Loch
there's a huge monster, or maybe even a
whole family of monsters, left over from the
days when dinosaurs ruled the earth.

Kevin MacAllister lived in a very old castle by the shores of Loch Ness. The castle was hundreds of years old and most of it had fallen down. But there were still lots of dark,

draughty rooms and a huge, winding stone staircase. Kevin was quite fit, because to get up to his bedroom he had to climb up 1239 steps. Sometimes he gave in half way up and went to sleep on the stairs instead.

passing wasp.

Kevin lived alone most of the time. His dad was a professional tramp, and so had to go away quite a lot, tramping. He tramped all over Scotland, sleeping on park benches, scratching himself on the bus in front of old ladies and stealing food from the pigeons in the town centre. At the time of our story (late autumn), Kevin's dad had just packed his plastic bag and gone off to the highlands for the Tramp Olympics. (He was representing Britain in the Two-man Snoring Event.) So Kevin was all alone in the family castle.

Well he wasn't quite alone. A few animals shared the place with him: there was Robertson the rook (his best friend), a bad tempered goat called Heidi, two tearaway cats, Rob and Roy, a spider called Robert the Bruce, and a family of bats who had never introduced themselves.

Alarm-clock so he can get up with the birds

Robertson enjoying a mug of Hot Chocolate before nest-time.

Chapter Two

One October morning, Kevin was sitting in his room, thinking of the Loch Ness monster. For as long as he could remember he'd wanted to be the first person to discover Nessie. And how long could he remember? About 30 centimetres.

But no matter how hard he wished, the monster never seemed to appear. Perhaps it was nervous – nervous as an ant walking down a street where anteaters live.

In one of the rooms of the castle (I can't remember exactly which one), Kevin had a telescope which looked out towards the Loch. It was so powerful you could count the hairs on a bluebottle's leg.

"Why do you bother?" croaked Robertson the rook. "You'll never see anything, no. No you won't."

Kevin didn't take any notice. He kept watching for any sign of life on the dark, deserted Loch.

10

Sometimes the waves looked like the tail of a great monster. And every so often the foam took on the appearance of a great dribbling sea creature. But where was the real Nessie? Tonight the moon was full and the Loch lay silvery bright, like a ten-pence piece in a tramp's wallet. An autumn wind was moaning through the trees. Rain splattered among the falling leaves and two squirrels shared a bar of Cadbury's Fruit and Nut.

Minutes turned into hours and still nothing moved across the Loch. It was as empty as a Rottweiler's Christmas stocking.

He could hear Heidi the goat in the room next door, eating a book of poetry (goats prefer eating poems to reading them).

Some tasty Roger McGough

'Munch'

"One last look," he thought, "and then I'm going to bed." And the thought of the 1239 steps turned his legs to jelly.

Orange flavour

Chapter Three

There was a sudden cry of "YIPPEEEE!" from the telescope room. It was so loud and unexpected that Rob and Roy ran off in a state of shock.

Out on Loch Ness a huge dark shadow was moving across the water like a torpedo with bumps. Kevin's heart began to thump. Loud as a car stereo with the bass full up. He didn't know whether to run down to the Loch, to search for his camera, or just to keep watching. It was the most exciting moment of his life, but unfortunately it didn't last long.

The "monster" hit a rock. And stood still. It wasn't a monster after all. It was the trunk of some rotten dead tree. Kevin felt like crying. Why couldn't the monster appear?

Perhaps it *didn't* exist. For the first time in his life, Kevin wasn't sure.

SPOT THE MONSTER (the Scottish eye test)

1. OLD TREE TRUNK ☒
2. GENUINE MONSTER ☑
3. SET OF OLD CAR TYRES ☒
4. SOME BIG WAVES ☒

Chapter Four

In a huge room at the top of 1239 steps,
Kevin lay in his sleeping bag while
Robertson the rook paced the floor:

Plonk, plonk, plonk . . .

"I can't get to sleep tonight, Kevin," he
croaked.

"Well try counting sheep."

"I don't like sheep."

"Then try something you do like.
Slugs . . . or worms."

Kevin gave a sigh and turned over with his head beneath the pillow. He heard a strange groaning sound. What on earth was it? Kevin pulled the pillow tighter over his head.

"Mooaaaa . . ."

Robertson flew up to the window ledge and looked out. "There's something down there, Kev . . . in the Loch. Come and take a loch, I mean take a look."

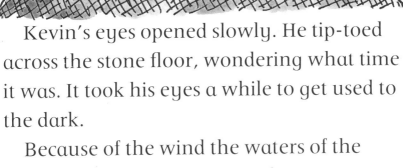

Kevin's eyes opened slowly. He tip-toed across the stone floor, wondering what time it was. It took his eyes a while to get used to the dark.

Because of the wind the waters of the Loch were choppy, and lots of waves were breaking on the shore.

"You sure it wasn't just a wave?" began Kevin, but before he could say anything else the head of a giant sea-creature suddenly rose out of the water. It gave a very loud cry, a bit like a seal with a loud-hailer. And then it disappeared back into the loch again. *Sploosh!*

Kevin raced around the room like a bluebottle finding a mouldy bun.

In the blink of an owl's eye he had run down the 1239 steps, out of the castle, and across the damp heathery hillside. He was heading towards Loch Ness.

"Don't go, Nessie!" he called out. "Just hold on a minute!"

Chapter Five

He found the Loch Ness monster lying
among some rocks close to the shore. By the
moonlight he could count each one of the
bumps on its shiny back. But after he'd done
that he couldn't really think of anything else
to do. Somehow it seemed rude to start
taking photographs. Especially since Nessie
was probably quite shy. She just lay there,
in the shallow water. Breathing softly.
Swishing her tail. She was like a giant silver
steam train.

Kevin took off his trainers and waded into the Loch. The water felt icy cold, but he didn't mind. This was the chance of a lifetime!

Chapter Six

Every night for the next week, Kevin would spend a few hours swimming and playing with Nessie. They always met at the same secret place, and quickly became the best of friends.

One fine autumn day, Kevin was walking out by the lochside, scrunching his feet through the golden leaves which were lying everywhere like giant cornflakes. He hummed a song to himself:

"Who is my friend?
You'll never guess,
I know the monster
Who lives in Loch Ness . . ."

Just then, someone shot out of the undergrowth and took a photograph. Kevin blinked in surprise. A short, sweaty man stepped forward to shake his hand. It was like shaking hands with a wet dish-cloth.

"Good morning, laddie," said the mysterious stranger. "My name is Elvis O'Bray. I'm a photographer on the *Abernoosty Times*." He raised his hat and mopped his brow with a grimy-looking handkerchief.

". . . Did I by any chance hear you mention the Loch Ness monster there?"

Kevin nodded. He didn't like the look of Mr O'Bray, but he was one of these people it's difficult to get away from.

Some other people KEVIN found it hard to get away from

ALISTAIR MURDOCH. Child maths genius. Once went on an arithmatic holiday

Mrs. McBain. Twice voted 'Nosiest Woman in Scotland.'

Neil Mackintosh. Small, red-haired and very irritating.

Mr. Plankton the postman. Sometimes bites dogs.

"Have you seen the monster recently?" continued the newspaperman. Kevin thought hard before admitting his story. But he hadn't seen anyone for ages and was bursting to tell his tale. Before long, Mr O'Bray was writing down the whole story. When he ran out of pages in his notebook he continued writing on the sleeve of his shirt, and then on the back of his hand.

O'Bray started to snigger like a hyena with a new joke book. "Tell me where I can photograph the monster and I'll give you fifty quid."

Kevin swallowed hard. Fifty pounds was a lot of money. At his present rate of pocket money it would take him nine years and four months to save that much. Fifty pounds! He could buy his dad a present: perhaps some string for his coat (tramps always fasten their coats with string). And a hundred other things he wanted. (I won't list them all because otherwise I might run out of ink before I can finish this story).

Mr O'Bray slapped Kevin on the back.
"Come on, laddie, I'm not going to hurt
your monster, just take a few snaps, that's
all. Give our readers a chance to see it. And
you'll be fifty quid better off."

For some reason Kevin felt he shouldn't tell Mr O'Bray about their secret place, but he did. The thought of all that money was just too much.

No sooner had Kevin described how to get to the spot than Mr O'Bray handed him fifty pounds and then ran off into the undergrowth chuckling to himself.

Kev looked at the fifty pounds and felt miserable.

He's blown it!

passing squirrel

Chapter Seven

As tea-time approached, Kevin was working at his desk. Robertson the rook flew into the room looking very upset. "Now you've done it! Now you've really done it!" squawked the great black bird, hopping around the room until dust flew everywhere.

"What d'you mean?" stammered Kevin.

"O'Bray the newspaperman is going to capture Nessie and sell her to a zoo!"

Kevin's heart sank. It sank like a biscuit dipped in hot tea.

"How d'you know?" he asked, angrily.

"I know because I was
sat on top of the
telephone box when
he rang his news-
paper friends.
He told them to
send an expert
at capturing large
wild beasts. Then he
rang the zoo and told them
they could buy the Loch Ness
monster for fifty thousand pounds."

Kevin's face turned beetroot red. This was all his fault. Unless he did something soon, Nessie would be captured by Elvis O'Bray. Imagine what a terrible life she'd have, stuck in a giant fish tank. Always on display. Never able to get a moment's peace.

The clock showed five-thirty in the afternoon. Time was running out!

Chapter Eight

"Hammer!"

"Clang!"

"Kerplunk!"

Strange noises were coming from Kevin's work-shed.

"Boing!"

"Zing!"

"Tap!"

Very strange noises.

An hour later Kevin opened the door of the shed and whistled to Robertson. The two of them began dragging a great long contraption out of the shed and down towards the water's edge. It was very heavy and noisy. Kevin hoped Elvis O'Bray wasn't around.

Chapter Nine

← Norman
the wildlife
expert

Elvis O'Bray and the wildlife expert were
standing by the spot where Kevin and
Nessie used to play. The wildlife expert was
called Norman. He was the sort of man who
used to wrestle with rhinos before breakfast.
And win! Elvis O'Bray took lots of snap-
shots, especially of Norman with his gun.

It was a fine clear night. Stars were shining like car headlights.

"What time is the monster supposed to appear?" asked Norman, who didn't really believe in this Loch Ness business.

"Any moment now," laughed the newspaperman, licking his lips. And sure enough, something had just drifted into sight on the other side of the Loch. It was huge and silvery and had a humped back . . .

Click click went O'Bray's camera. He was so excited the camera shook. Norman's finger was ready on the trigger of his gun. One good shot with a tranquillizing dart would send the monster to sleep for at least an hour.

That would give them loads of time to drag it ashore and on to their lorry.

Where was Kevin? Why hadn't he tried to warn his friend?

Chapter Ten

Norman had just got Nessie into the sights of
his gun when he noticed her head. It looked
very like an old dustbin. In fact it *was* an old
dustbin. Not only that, but her body too was
made from bits of old scrap metal held
together with a length of hosepipe.

Elvis O'Bray was furious. "It's a hoax! That rotten kid tricked me!"

His companion couldn't help but laugh. "I knew it couldn't be true. There's no such thing as the Loch Ness monster. It serves me right for listening to a chump like you, O'Bray."

The false Nessie (the one Kevin had made in his workshed), had now run aground. O'Bray and Norman could quite clearly make out the collection of old dustbins, a broom handle, two empty oil drums, and the front lights off a Mini Metro.

O'Bray muttered miserably all the way home. So much so that poor Norman had to switch the car radio onto full volume. He would rather have driven home with a rhino than with moaning Elvis O'Bray.

Kevin ran out from the bushes where he'd been hiding and yelled at the top of his voice. (The top of your voice is a good place to yell from.) "YAHOOO!"

Radio times

The model monster had done the trick. O'Bray had been completely fooled and no longer believed in the monster. He would probably tell the zoo it had all been a cruel hoax.

Robertson the rook landed on top of one of the floating dustbins and gave a cough.

"Now, Kev, since I helped you out I think you should return Mr O'Bray's fifty pounds, because you didn't really earn it. If you like I can drop it into his office tomorrow 'cos I'm flying over that way."

Kevin nodded his head.

". . . And secondly," continued the rook, "I think it's time I was introduced to the real Nessie. I've always wanted to meet a monster."

Chapter Eleven

Kevin wondered if Nessie would ever show her humps again. It was a terrible thing he'd done, breaking a secret and giving away the hiding place. He still felt pretty guilty.

He looked at his waterproof watch. Nessie was ten minutes late, and Robertson was beginning to look a little down in the beak.

In the distance there came a faint *sploosh*. The waves on the Loch grew larger. A seagull flew off looking extremely worried.

"Moooah!"

There was Nessie paddling towards them, silvery humps on her back, tail swishing beneath the stars. Kevin thought he could see a smile across her scaly sea-monster face. Robertson the rook hopped on to Kev's shoulder and gave a croak of delight: "Croak! Its the real thing!"

So you see the Loch Ness monster really does exist, and if you don't believe me you can always take a trip up to Loch Ness and see for yourself. Just look for a spot near the tumbledown old castle. I'm sure you'll see *some*thing . . .

* Oh yes, no doubt about it!

Look out for other exciting new titles in the **Red Storybooks** series.

Thomas and the Tinners
Jill Paton Walsh
Illustrated by Alan Marks

Thomas works in the tin mine where he meets some fairy miners who cause him a great deal of trouble – but then bring him good fortune.

Dreamy Daniel, Brainy Bert
Scoular Anderson

Daniel is a daydreamer and is always getting into trouble at school. But with the help of Bert, the class mouse, Daniel proves that he's just as capable as anyone else in the class!

Hopping Mad
Nick Warburton
Illustrated by Tony Blundell

Janey's daft little brother, Martin, is daft, clumsy and useless. But one day Janey discovers his one talent – he's brilliant at jumping around in a duvet cover. Why not enter Martin for the big pillow race at sports day?

The Saracen Maid
Leon Garfield
Illustrated by John Talbot

Young Gilbert Beckett is captured by pirates and sold to a rich Arab merchant. But the merchant's beautiful daughter falls in love with Gilbert and promises to help him escape . . .

You can buy all these books from your local bookshop, or they can be ordered direct from the publishers. For more information about Storybooks write to The Sales Department, Macdonald Young Books Ltd, Campus 400, Maylands Avenue, Hemel Hempstead HP2 7EZ.